Dinosaurs

Apatosaurus

by Julie Murray

Dash!
LEVELED READERS
An Imprint of Abdo Zoom • abdobooks.com

Level 1 – Beginning
Short and simple sentences with familiar words or patterns for children who are beginning to understand how letters and sounds go together.

Level 2 – Emerging
Longer words and sentences with more complex language patterns for readers who are practicing common words and letter sounds.

Level 3 – Transitional
More developed language and vocabulary for readers who are becoming more independent.

abdobooks.com

Published by Abdo Zoom, a division of ABDO, PO Box 398166, Minneapolis, Minnesota 55439.
Copyright © 2023 by Abdo Consulting Group, Inc. International copyrights reserved in all countries.
No part of this book may be reproduced in any form without written permission from the publisher.
Dash!™ is a trademark and logo of Abdo Zoom.

Printed in China
052022
092022

Photo Credits: Alamy, Getty Images, Shutterstock
Production Contributors: Kenny Abdo, Jennie Forsberg, Grace Hansen, John Hansen
Design Contributors: Candice Keimig, Neil Klinepier

Library of Congress Control Number: 2021950310

Publisher's Cataloging in Publication Data

Names: Murray, Julie, author.
Title: Apatosaurus / by Julie Murray
Description: Minneapolis, Minnesota : Abdo Zoom, 2023 | Series: Dinosaurs | Includes online resources and index.
Identifiers: ISBN 9781098228279 (lib. bdg.) | ISBN 9781098229115 (ebook) | ISBN 9781098229535 (Read-to-Me ebook)
Subjects: LCSH: Apatosaurus--Juvenile literature. | Dinosaurs--Juvenile literature. | Paleontology--Juvenile literature. | Extinct animals--Juvenile literature.
Classification: DDC 567.90--dc23

Table of Contents

Apatosaurus

Apatosaurus was a **sauropod**. It lived over 150 million years ago.

It likely lived near riverbanks.
There it could find both trees
and water.

Apatosaurus was huge. It was one of the largest animals to ever walk the Earth!

It could grow up to 75 feet (23 m) long. It weighed up to 70,000 pounds (31,751.5 kg)!

Its tail was very long!
It was used like a whip
for **defense**.

12

Apatosaurus walked on four legs. The front legs were shorter than the back.

Apatosaurus had a long neck. It could reach leaves high up in trees.

Apatosaurus laid eggs. Each
egg could measure 5 feet
(1.5 m) in length!

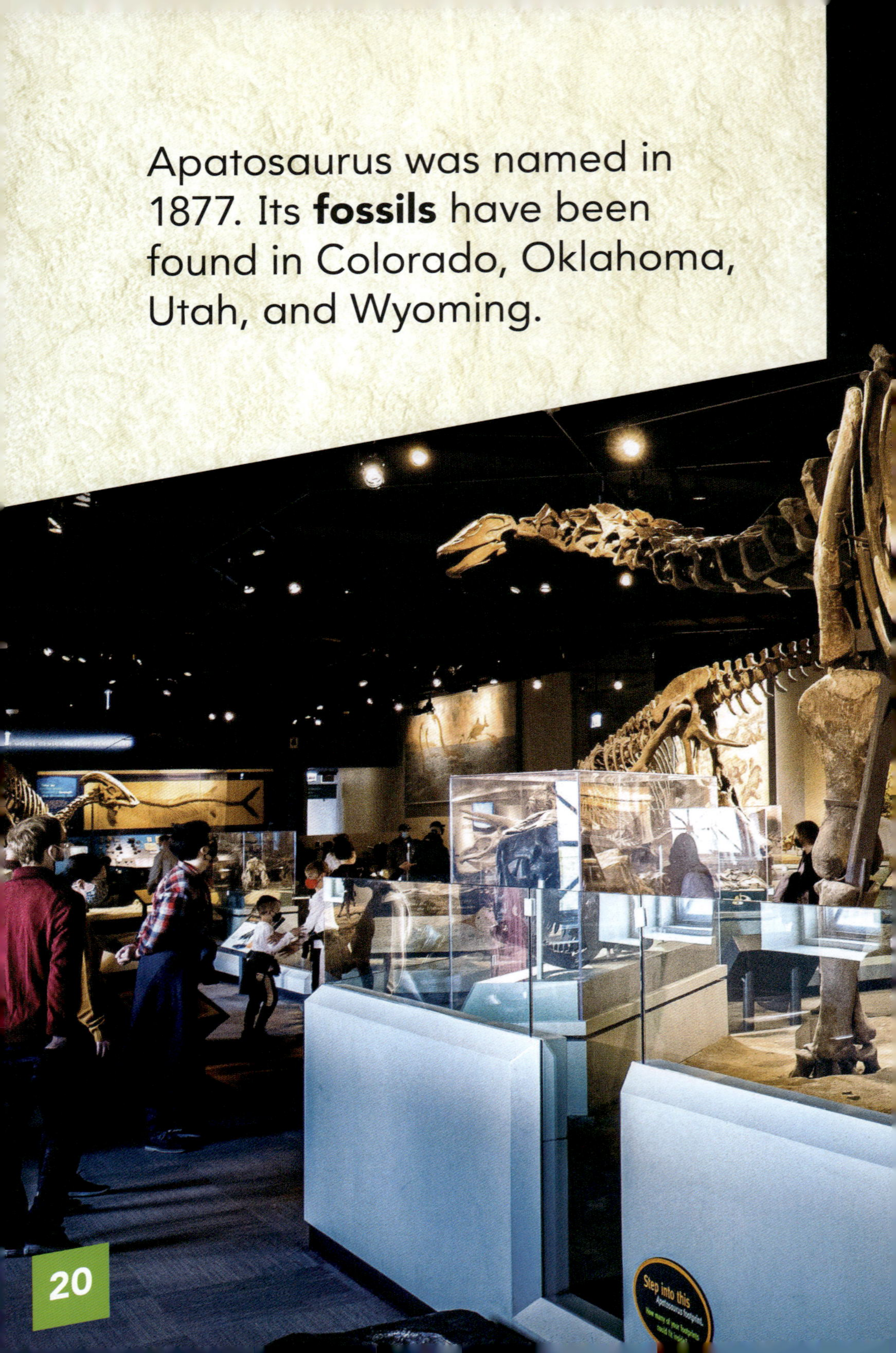

Apatosaurus was named in 1877. Its **fossils** have been found in Colorado, Oklahoma, Utah, and Wyoming.

- Some scientists believe that Apatosaurus laid its eggs as it walked, instead of in a nest.

- Apatosaurus only ate plants. It ate up to 800 pounds (362.9 kg) of food each day!

- It lived to be 100 years old or more.

Glossary

defense – to protect or guard.

fossil – the remains or trace of a living animal or plant from a long time ago. Fossils are found embedded in earth or rock.

sauropod – a very large, four-legged, plant-eating dinosaur of a group whose members have a long neck and tail, small head, and massive limbs.

Index

Online Resources

Booklinks
NONFICTION NETWORK
FREE! ONLINE NONFICTION RESOURCES

To learn more about Apatosaurus, please visit **abdobooklinks.com** or scan this QR code. These links are routinely monitored and updated to provide the most current information available.